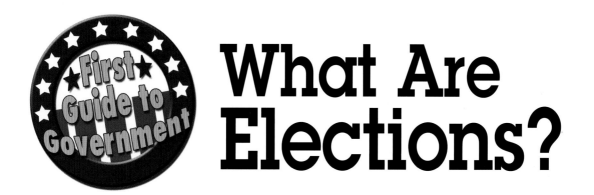

What Are Elections?

Nancy Harris

Heinemann Library
Chicago, Illinois

Customer Service 888-454-2279
Visit our website at **www.heinemannlibrary.com**

Designed by Kimberly R. Miracle and Betsy Wernert
Photo Research by Tracy Cummins and Tracey Engel
Maps provided by Map Specialists
Printed in China by South China Printing Company

11 10 09 08 07
10 9 8 7 6 5 4 3 2 1

ISBN-10: 1-4034-9469-X (hc)   1-4034-9475-4 (pb)

Library of Congress Cataloging-in-Publication Data
Harris, Nancy, 1956-
   What are elections? / Nancy Harris.
       p. cm. -- (First guide to government)
   Includes bibliographical references and index.
   ISBN-13: 978-1-4034-9469-6 (hc)
   ISBN-13: 978-1-4034-9475-7 (pb)
   1. Elections--United States--Juvenile literature. I. Title.
JK1978.H37 2007
324.60973--dc22

                              2007003267

Acknowledgments
The author and publishers are grateful to the following for permission to reproduce copyright material: Alamy **pp. 4** (Glow
Images), **8** (Jeff Greenberg), **9** (Jeff Greenberg), **10** (SCPhotos), **29** (Richard Levine); AP Photo **pp. 5** (Ron Edmonds),
7 (Robert F. Bukaty), **14** (Phelan M. Ebenhack), **19** (Charles Bennett) **23** (Bob Child), **25** (Jeff Gentner); Corbis **pp.**
11 (Shawn Thew/epa), **21** (Owen Franken); Getty Images **pp. 6** (ROBYN BECK/AFP), **12** (Joe Raedle), **13** (Craig
Mitchelldyer), **15** (AFP/GABRIEL BOUYS), **17** (Alex Wong), **20** (AFP/STEPHEN JAFFE), **24** (Scott Olson), **27** (AFP/GABRIEL
BOUYS); Landov **pp. 18** (Reuters/CHIP EAST), **22** (UPI/KEVIN DIETSCH); Reuters **pp. 26** (CORBIS), **28** (CORBIS).

Cover photograph reproduced with permission of Mike Simons/Getty Images.

Contents

Some words are shown in bold, **like this**. You can find out what they mean by looking in the glossary.

What Is Government?

The United States **federal government** runs the country. It is a **democracy**. This means it is made up of leaders who are **elected** (chosen) to run the country.

★ The federal government is in Washington, D.C.

Many people work in the federal government. They represent the wishes of all the **citizens** of the United States. Citizens are people who live in the United States and can vote for their leaders.

These people work in the part of the government that makes **laws** (rules).

What Are Elections?

Elections are days when **citizens** can vote to choose leaders in the government. Citizens **elect** leaders in the **federal government**. They also elect leaders in their state and local (smaller) governments.

★ This man is voting to choose leaders in government.

★ People mark who they want as leaders on a ballot.

Citizens choose a person for each leadership position from a list. The list is called a **ballot**. It has the names of all the people who are running for each position. The **candidates** who get the most votes win.

Who Can Vote?

★ These men have just become American citizens.

There are **laws** that say who can vote in the United States. You must be eighteen years old or older to vote. You must also be a **citizen** of the United States. You must live in a state for a certain period of time to vote in that state.

People must **register** (sign up) to vote before an election. They can do so at a voter registration office in their city. They can also register by filling out a form and sending it in the mail.

Booths are set up in neighborhoods to make it easier to register to vote.

Where Do You Vote?

Places are set up where people can vote. These are called **polling places**. They are usually set up in public buildings in neighborhoods.

★ People are sent a notice that tells them the location of their polling place.

⭐ Election inspectors have a list of registered voters.

Each polling place has election inspectors. They check to see if each person has **registered** to vote. Once they find a person's name on the list, they ask that person to sign in. He or she can then vote.

How Do You Vote?

After a person has signed in, he or she is taken to a booth to vote. Then the person looks over the **ballot** carefully.

★ Voting booths are divided so that people can make their choice in private.

The ballot has the list of all the people running for different leadership positions. People vote for one person for each leadership position.

On some paper ballots, people fill in a bubble to mark their choice.

★ Paper ballots are locked in a box until they are counted.

People do not put their name on the **ballot**. Their vote is kept secret. The votes are counted at the end of the day.

Newspapers name the winners after enough votes have been counted.

The votes are made public that evening. The winners are announced on the radio, television, Internet, and in the newspaper. The winners will become the new leaders.

National Elections

November

Sunday	Monday	Tuesday	Wednesday	Thursday	Friday	Saturday
						1
2	3	4	5	6	7	8
9	10	11	12	13	14	15
16	17	18	19	20	21	22
23	24	25	26	27	28	29
30						

National elections are elections for leaders in the **federal government**. These leaders make decisions for the whole country. National elections are held on the Tuesday after the first Monday in November.

National elections include voting for:

- president
- vice president
- **senators**
- **representatives**.

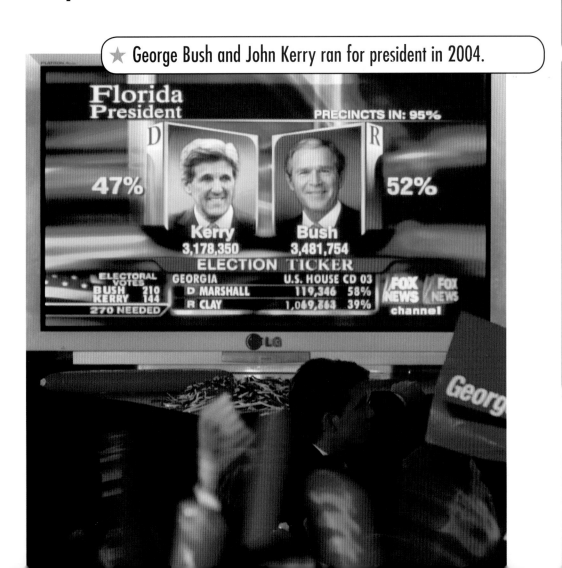

★ George Bush and John Kerry ran for president in 2004.

Voting for President and Vice President

Every four years, people vote for president and vice president of the United States. Presidential **candidates** choose the person they want to be vice president. The president and vice president are **elected** as a pair.

PRESS OUT CIRCLED CROSS(ES) ⊕ TO VOTE
VOTER DETACH AND KEEP THIS STUB.

MECKLENBURG COUNTY   **11/02/04**

SEPARATE VOTE
PRESIDENT / VICE PRESIDENT
(YOU MAY VOTE FOR ONE)

JOHN F. KERRY/JOHN EDWARDS	DEM ➤	+
GEORGE W. BUSH/DICK CHENEY	REP ➤	+
MICHAEL BADNARIK/RICHARD CAMPAGNA	LIB ➤	+
WRITE-IN	➤	+

STRAIGHT PARTY VOTE
(YOU MAY VOTE FOR ONE)

➤ | +

This **ballot** lists the candidates for president and vice president in 2004.

People can vote only for one pair of candidates. The winners will be the new leaders of the country.

OFFICIAL BALLOT (BALOTA OFICIAL)

RESIDENT AND VICE PRESIDENT OF THE UNITED STATES
PRESIDENTE Y VICE PRESIDENTE DE LOS ESTADOS UNIDOS

VOTE FOR ONE GROUP
VOTE POR UN GRUPO

EORGE W. BUSH AND DICK CHENEY	REPUBLICAN	2 →
L GORE AND JOE LIEBERMAN	DEMOCRATIC	4 →
RRY BROWNE AND ART OLIVIER	LIBERTARIAN	6 →
LPH NADER AND WINONA LaDUKE	GREEN	8 →
HN HAGELIN AND NAT GOLDHABER	REFORM	10 →
BUCHANAN AND EZOLA FOSTER	INDEPENDENT	12 →

NTATIVE IN CONGRESS 1ST CONGRESSIONAL DISTRICT
ENTANTE EN CONGRESO 1er DISTRITO CONGRESIONAL

VOTE FOR ONE
VOTE POR UNO

| MOND G. WARDINGLEY | REPUBLICAN | 18 → |
| BY L. RUSH | DEMOCRATIC | 20 → |

TURN PAGE
TO CONTINUE
VOTING

OLTEE LA
GINA
TINUAR
DO

★★★ Some ballots have holes you must punch through in order to select your choice.

Who Can Run for President?

★ George W. Bush was elected president in 2000 and 2004.

There are rules that say who can run for president.
The rules are:

- You must be born in the United States.
- You must be at least 35 years old.
- You must have lived in the United States for at least 14 years.

Who Can Run for Vice President?

There are rules that say who run for vice president. These rules are the same as the rules for the president.

The president and vice president can be **elected** twice. They can serve a total of eight years together.

President Jimmy Carter and Vice President Walter Mondale served together from January 1977 to January 1981.

Voting for a Senator

Citizens vote for members of **Congress**. Congress is where **laws** (rules) are made. A **senator** works in the part of Congress called the Senate.

★ Hillary Rodham Clinton is a senator from New York.

22

★ Joe Lieberman has been **elected** senator of Connecticut four times.

Each state has two senators. People in each state vote for their own senators. They can go to a **polling place** to vote.

23

Who Can Run for Senator?

★ Barack Obama was elected senator of Illinois in 2004.

There are rules that tell who can run for **senator**. The rules are:

- You must be at least 30 years old.
- You must be a United States **citizen** for nine years before your election.
- You must live in the state you are representing during the time of the election.

★★★ Robert Byrd is the longest-serving senator in history. He has been in office since 1959.

A senator serves (works) for six years and then can be **elected** again. There is no limit to how many times a senator can be elected.

Voting for a Representative

Representatives also work in **Congress**, the part of government that makes **laws**. They work in the House of Representatives.

These representatives serve in Congress.
They help make laws.

Each state has at least one representative. People vote only for their state's representatives. They can go to a **polling place** to vote.

Polling places are often set up at schools, libraries, or fire stations.

Who Can Run for Representative?

There are rules that tell who can run for **representative**. The rules are:

- You must be at least 25 years old.
- You must be a United States **citizen** for seven years before your election.
- You must live in the state you are representing during the time of the election.

Representatives serve for two years and then can run for office again.

Why Is Voting Important?

Elections are an important part of our country. They mean that citizens get to choose their leaders. This is what makes our government a **democracy**.

In a democracy, all citizens are represented in government.

Glossary

ballot list of all the people running for leadership positions

candidate person who is running for a leadership position

citizen person who is born in the United States. People who have moved to the United States from another country can become citizens by taking a test.

Congress place where laws (rules) are made. Congress has two houses: the Senate and the House of Representatives. It is part of the United States federal government.

democracy country that is run by leaders who are elected by the people in the country

elect choose a person to be a leader by voting

federal government government where a group of leaders runs the entire country. In a federal government, the country is made up of many states. The United States is a federal government.

law rule people must obey in a state or country

national election election for people who work in the federal government

polling place place where people go to vote

register sign up to vote

representative member of Congress who works in the House of Representatives. Congress is where laws are made.

senator member of Congress who works in the Senate. Congress is where laws are made.

Ways People Vote in the United States

paper ballots Voters mark their choices for leaders using a pencil.

punchcards Voters punch a hole next to their choice for a leader.

mechanical lever machines Voters pull down a lever to mark their choice for leader.

marksense Voters mark their choices using a pencil. The votes are counted by a computer scanning the votes.

DRE Voting Machine Voters mark their choices on a computer screen.

absentee ballot People mail their vote before the election because they cannot go to a polling place on the day of the election.

More Books to Read

An older reader can help you with these books:
Christelow, Eileen. *Vote!* New York: Clarion Books, 2003.

Murphy, Patricia J. *Election Day.* Memorial, NY: Children's Press, 2002.

Murphy, Patricia J. *Voting and Elections.* Mankato, MN: Compass Point Books, 2002.

Index